THE ART OF MOTHER HOOD

ART, POETRY AND MEMOIRS OF A POSTPARTUM JOURNEY

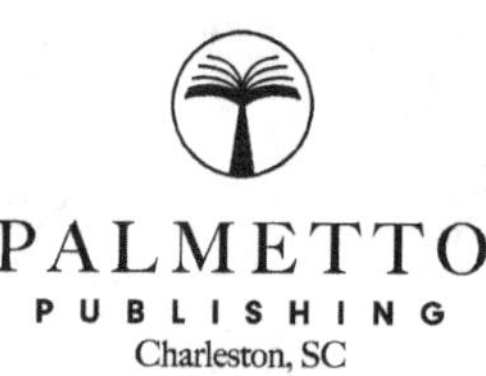

PALMETTO

PUBLISHING

Charleston, SC
www.PalmettoPublishing.com

Paperback ISBN: 979-8-8229-5449-6
eBook ISBN: 979-8-8229-5450-2

THE ART OF MOTHER HOOD

ART, POETRY AND MEMOIRS OF A POSTPARTUM JOURNEY

NATASHA K. PRECKAJLO

Dedication

For My Boys:
Oliver, Elliott & Justin,
I hope always to make you proud.
I Love you.

And for all the amazing women in my life who have
inspired me: This is for you.

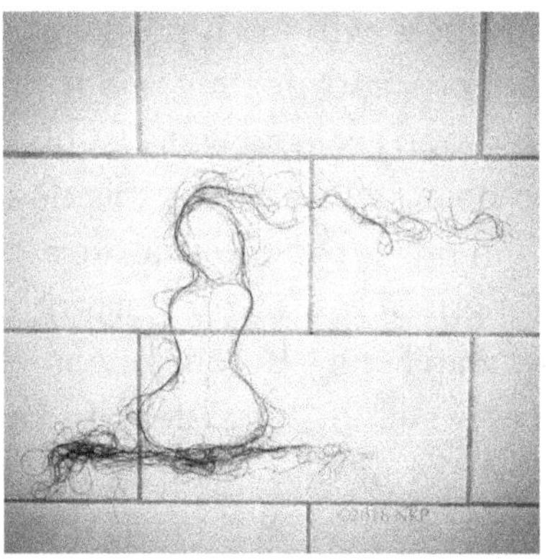

"Sweet Serenity"

Introduction

In 2018 after the birth of my first son, I felt the sharp void of a life lost. A mother was born and in an instant the life that once was ceased to exist. I had the same life style, job, friends, house, but I was forever changed- my life had greatly shifted. Slowly, though I started to find some solace, some sense of self again...and it all started with an odd project spurred on by a postpartum symptom, and some time alone in the shower. For those of you who haven't heard of or had the "pleasure" of experiencing postpartum mass hair shedding: Yes, it's a real thing, and thankfully my hair did come back. The upside to the hair loss was an unexpected creative outlet that turned into a yearlong art project. How did I discover this "medium" you may ask? Having long hair, as I've had for most of my life, I became accustomed to slapping my random sheadings on the shower wall as you do. Right?! I guarantee any woman or man with long hair who doesn't want to regularly snake the drain, knows exactly what I'm talking about. One day while my son was napping and I had the rare chance to take a shower by myself I thought, "Hey how funny would it be if I could actually make a picture out of all this hair I leave on the wall." So, I decided what the

1

hell...let's do it. Armed with my iPhone I started taking pictures of my creations and posting them on Facebook and Instagram. What I soon realized was just how much I needed this. I needed to be able to express this deep-seated desire to center myself in my newfound skin, as a mother. Just that little time, the length of a shower, started to bring me back to myself- the woman I knew before becoming a mother. The woman I knew was still in there despite the shift into this uncharted territory of my life. With all my energy, love and care going to someone else, and least of all myself, this was the one way I was able to fill my cup. I began to realize if I was feeling this way, I could not be the only one out there experiencing this; feeling this overwhelming shift and not knowing how to come back to self, to center and wanting to feel like support was there waiting for me. That primal need is what eventually led me to start my LLC, MyTrybe. Which is focused on being a holistic support for mothers and women.

What my experience really highlighted though, was the importance of mothers not losing ourselves in the pursuit of caring for our children. I truly believe that if we are supported and continue to thrive as the amazing women we were before, and after motherhood, then we can achieve the most amazing of things... and that is what I find to be the truest magic of all.

So, this is my creative ode to those first years of postpartum life, and to the woman I became and am continuing to become. I hope you enjoy this journey that I went on and I hope, if you are on a similar one, that it brings you some peace to know you are not alone, and you can and will find your way back to you again.

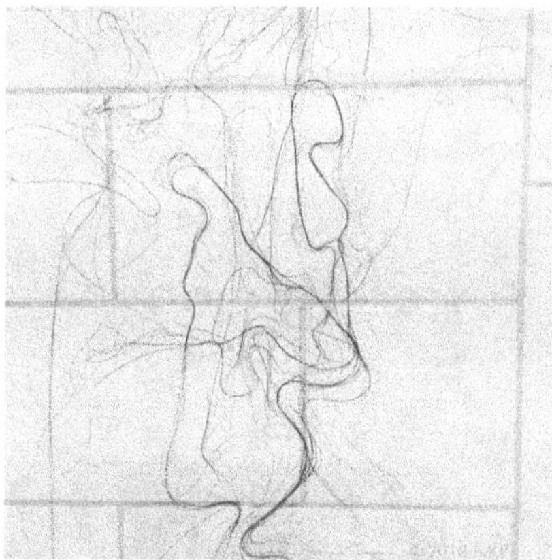

"Untitled"

This was one of the first pieces I created. I love the movement in the piece. I put it on Facebook and asked, "What do you see here?"... and I again ask: What do you see? Better yet, what does this make you feel?

Part 1
Transformation

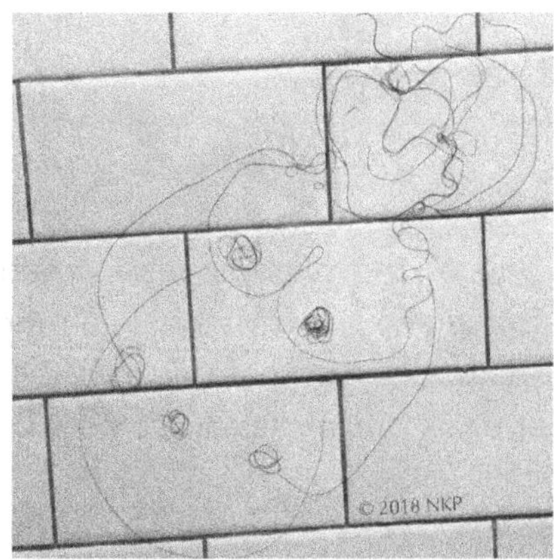

"My Growing Garden"

Right before my first son was born, I remember making a bucket list, as I think maybe a lot of us do at some point along the way...All the things we want to do one day. I remember number 45 on the list was "pose nude for a figure drawing class." Of course, that would mean I had the gumption to be nude in front of so many people...because that would mean I felt comfortable enough in my skin, not to hide, or be anything less than at easy or confident. Fast forward 4 years and I eventually checked that off my bucket list. I was pregnant with my second son at the time. And somehow this time, this pregnancy, I felt ready. I felt more like I finally was truly living in my skin; this was me... nothing to hold back. I relished in my pregnant body and I felt more at home, alive and glorious in that state than in any other I had felt since. Maybe it was because I had been here before, pregnant, and knew what it felt like. Or maybe it was because after having given birth once, before it didn't feel so shameful anymore, everyone had already seen the goods. Whatever it was, it was intoxicating. Empowering. All the artists were marveling over the fact that I was doing this pregnant, and how it was such a special thing. Damn right it was! I loved my body more in those times than I ever had before in my life; not just because it was able to hold life; but because I finally felt free, free of the pressure to be thin or to be sexy or whatever else society puts on you as a woman. I felt free to eat (healthy amounts- but still) I felt free to just be! I loved how full my hair was (ironic because we know how that went) I loved the glow...even if that was sweat from being out of breath. But most of all, I loved the quiet in my mind. Pregnancy hormones, after the first trimester that is, allowed my anxiety to subside. I know this is not always the case in pregnancy, as anxieties can be stirred. But for me it was the opposite. Which is why when my husband suggested, "Hey maybe you should model for the figure drawing class now...how cool would it be to do it pregnant?! Might be your only chance to do it." I jumped at the opportunity. And if anxieties were going to be stirred... oh man, this would have been the time! I was up there for over an hour and a half. Honestly though after the first pose, I took my glasses off and everything just settled in. I even started to dose off in the last pose.

What pregnancy helped me learn though was to love my body, to honor the magnificent ability that I was given in this form and to be proud of all it can do. How powerful it truly is to be a creator.

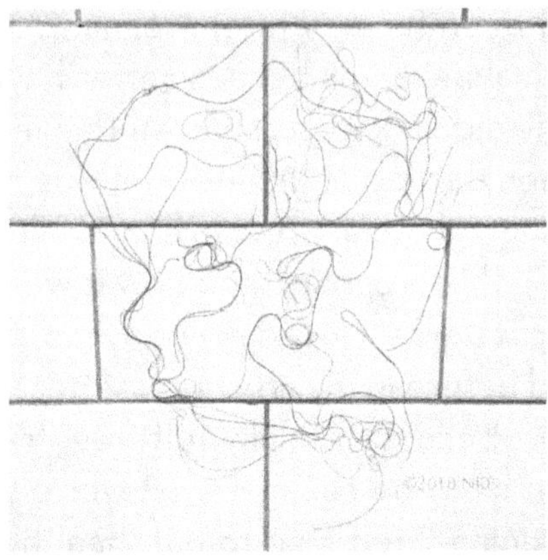

"The Sprite"

<u>Changing</u>

Like a nymph or a wily sprite, she began to change to her hearts delight. Not just in form but internally too.She was not the maiden from before, who was long since passed. Though was she still there? The echoes of her essence still lurking in the shadows. Would she resurface or was she destined to remain in the past? In the questioning a hit of fear in the thought. Deep inside she awaits; awaits her return, maybe she has morphed into someone else; someone new. Her friends of old have faded with the seasons. Not exactly sure why but she knows there were reasons. Others rise up taking their place, the space in her heart full now, replaced. The loss is mourned, know that to be true, yet some are for a reason, a season or a lifetime. Holding dear to the future now, for what's to come. The past is the past and that's all we can ask. The changing, ever constant, ever real, for it is the beauty and the pain in this life. And for that we must all feel.

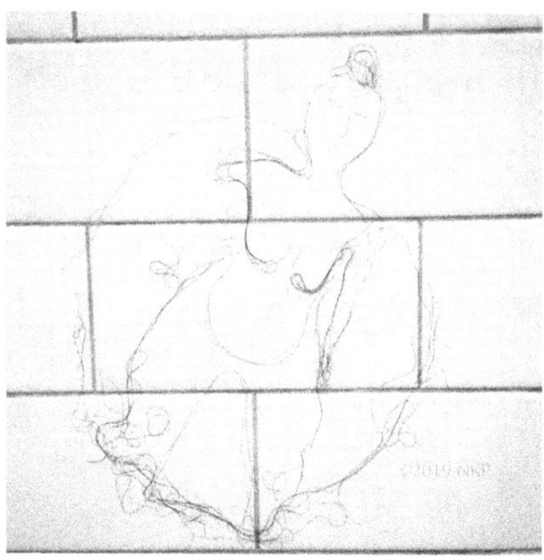

"Labor of Love"

The Mother of All

She creeped in subtly ever so softly. She could feel my apprehension, my fear of letting go and letting her in. She held my hand and cooed in my ear lulling me to soften my tense muscles and locked jaw. She said "its ok, my sweet you have been strong for so long, its ok to open, to allow for life to come forth." She held me close and rocked me urging my body to supple, urging me to bloom and open. She wiped my brow and held me tight and when," I can't! No more" She was there all the more. I don't know her name, I don't know her story but She is the everywhere, the everywoman the wisdom of ages. She is the rising of the tides, the innate, the winds of eternity. The sky, the stars, the mother earth, She is the magic of life, and She breathed through me. I shall not doubt again for She is within me. Passed down and handed over at birth- She is my right, my ritual, my wisdom and glory. She is sacred and wise. Steadfast and warm, She is there for you always. "*I See you,*" She says, and you have never been fuller, more whole, you are not weak or small; unable to do this. You ARE doing this.

You are this. It is so.

"I know, "she says, "For I see your heart and soul, and it is fiercely mother earth, it is divinely feminine! You my love are the moon and all the stars, nor have you ever been more breath taking, than as you give the breath of life."

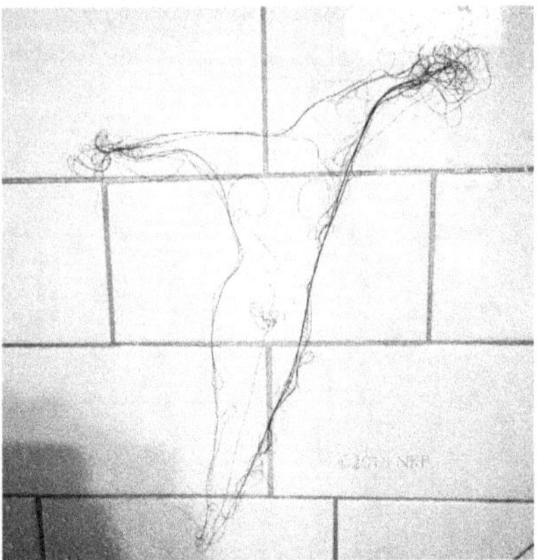

"The Feminine Within"

Both of my boys were born in a birth center, and both were water births. I opted for natural deliveries as that's how my mother had me and my grandmother had most of her children. I felt I could do it, I always had a sense I could do it, that my body was made for this and all I had to do was trust. Trust that my body would just do its thing. I am grateful that it did and grateful that I had the support of my doula, husband, midwives, mother and best friend (who literally jumped on a plane from New York the morning I was in labor, just to be there for the birth of my first son.) Having so many people around me who believed I could do this, fortified me.

Although, not everyone was in support of my choices. I was met with some naysayers; mostly men but some women, and more surprising still, some female physicians. Most said, "Why do you want to go through the pain? What are you trying to prove? You will just ruin your vagina. C-sections are safer for the mother, and the baby." "The List" went on; In the end I had to tell someone close to me, that this was not their choice, they didn't get a vote. This was my birth and how I would choose to bring life into the world. Not them,

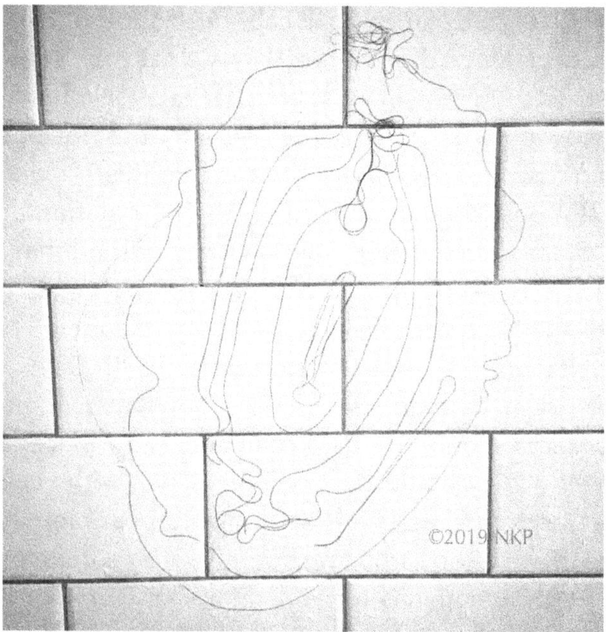

"My take, on Georgia"

not the doctor at Mayo who said this, that, or the other, but me. And if the time came for extraordinary measures, that would be between me and my husband (but still mostly me.)

Trust, for me, is the biggest part of the natal process. Women trusting their bodies, and not being made to feel they should fear them. In me saying this, I don't mean that every woman should or must have an unmedicated birth. Nor that if her birth doesn't look like someone else's, then there is something wrong with her or her experience. In fact, a close friend of mine, opted for a medicated birth because SHE knew that her body and her mind would relax. And when it did, then she could do the "marathon" of work that lay ahead of her. It was because she knew her body so well, that ultimately, she knew what would work for her.

What I am saying is that there needs to be less fear and more empowerment around birth. More body awareness, knowing your body and what it calls for. It's you who has been IN your body since day one, you know what your body needs best. I trusted in that, in what I felt. If that would have had to change, I would have made the decision, but not because I was told to doubt myself or "you can't do this." I would have made the best decision based on the information at hand, not because the naysayers said one way or the other.

Providers who support women and their right to advocate for the birth they want should be applauded; My hope is that women who chose to experience birth the way they want to, are made to feel safe and empowered in their choices. For birth should not be a traumatic experience for anyone involved, it should be one that is met with reverence, support and care as much as humanly possible. How did your birth shape how you feel about your experience? Think back...did it alter things for you? Make you feel one way or the other? Birth can change us and often does...How does reflecting on your experience, good bad or indifferent feel now?

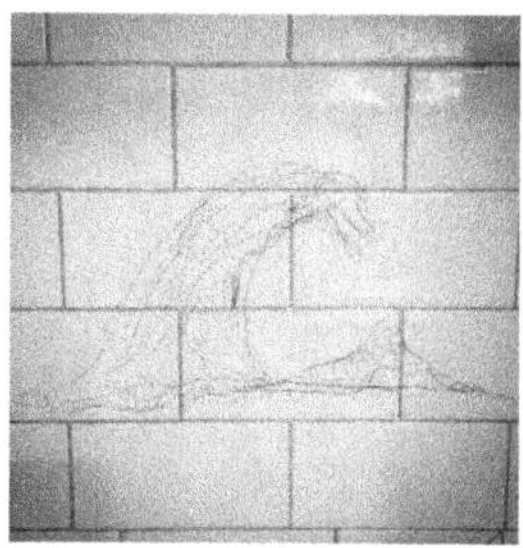

"Wavy Locks"

<u>Thoughts on Motherhood</u>
Alone in the night, up with only my thoughts and a tiny little
soul for company....
What is this kind of love that never quits; that is there even
when they are gone, gone to an endless world of dreams
and sweet dewy slumber.
The kind of love that washes over you like a tidal wave
engulfing your heart and leaving you wrecked on the shores
of parenthood.
What is this love that enables a woman to endure hours
upon hours of physical transformation... transformation
from that of maiden to mother, in an instant
One gone and another remains,
One gone who is known and one remains who is as newly
born as her babe.
As I sit here holding your hand in mine, I know not how I
could love you more. You my child, my greatest creation,
you shan't understand the depths of my adoration.
No... not yet. But please know that like you I am new, I am
learning, my love never yielding,
but please be gentle when you think of mummy
for she too was freshly forged, as you once were and
though she loved you she may have mis stepped, mistook.
But as I sit with you now in your dream world,
know that I am here.
Your rock and protector.
Your mother
Now and forever.

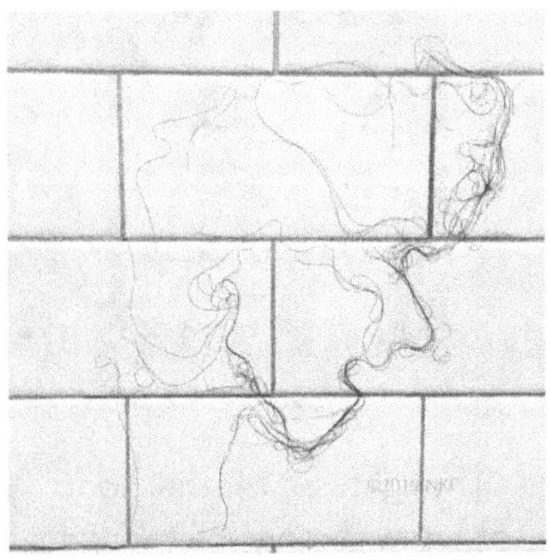

"Anna's Fall"

<u>A Mother's Cry</u>
I once heard a woman say
To Be mother is a job like no other,
it is thankless and hard
fraught with pain and sorrow.
But be sure that nothing would make her
tomorrow more joyous than the
smile and warm
embrace of the child that God
granted she grace.
For even now at the end of the day
with dishes piled high
and dirt all upon her face.
She is never more needed or loved
than by the small hearts
that beat in their beds.
Her cry of weariness
and solitude
is one that connects
her to the others
for no one can understand
the cry of a mother
quite like another.

Part 2
The Journey

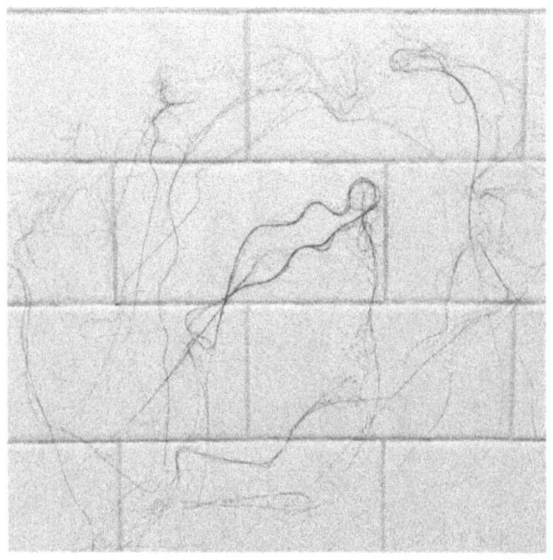

"Botticelli Babe"

As a lover of art, and someone who was in the National Art Honors society in high school (not that, that meant much other than I loved painting and drawing and I really wanted the rainbow tassel and cords for graduation.) I knew enough about some of the great master artists and painters of history... and was it, Picasso who said "good artist borrow and great artist steal"? I can't remember... What you will notice with a lot of my hair art (h.art if you will) is that it really focuses on the female form and archetypes. I think it's really how I was able to connect with the transformation from maiden to mother that I went through in my postpartum journey.

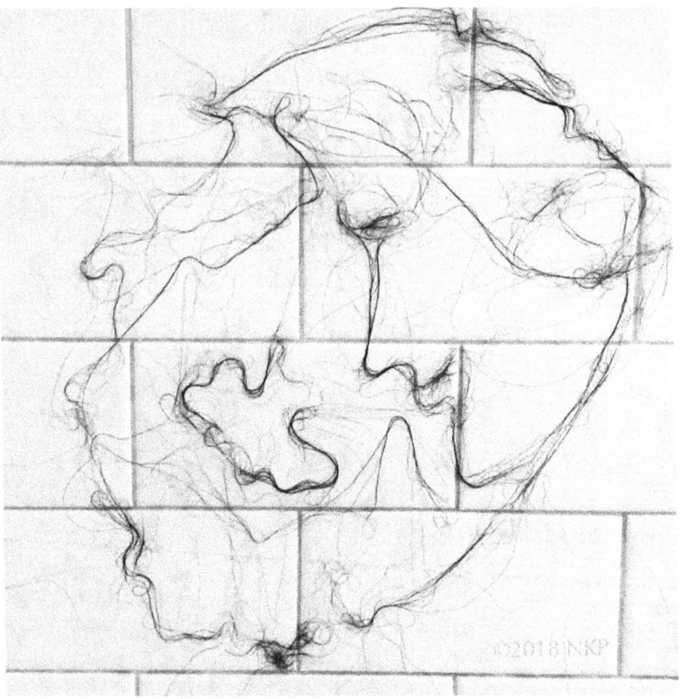

"Moon Mother"

For the longest time "Moon Mother" was one of my favorite pieces, I love the way she is looking down at her little blob, her creation; be it the earth and she the moon or her newly formed babe in her womb. She is the mother, the feminine, the moon, her cool light shining downward, but also inward. Her pull, on the tides, as women we cycle with her. She is mystical and magical, and because of this I have always loved her (and the sun). The relationship of the two celestial orbs has always fascinated me; Just like star crossed lovers. They oscillate in each other's orbit, at times meeting briefly. On a full moon night, I would go outside after the little one was asleep and just bask in her light. Just the silence of the night and her clear bright light, made me feel connected to something more.

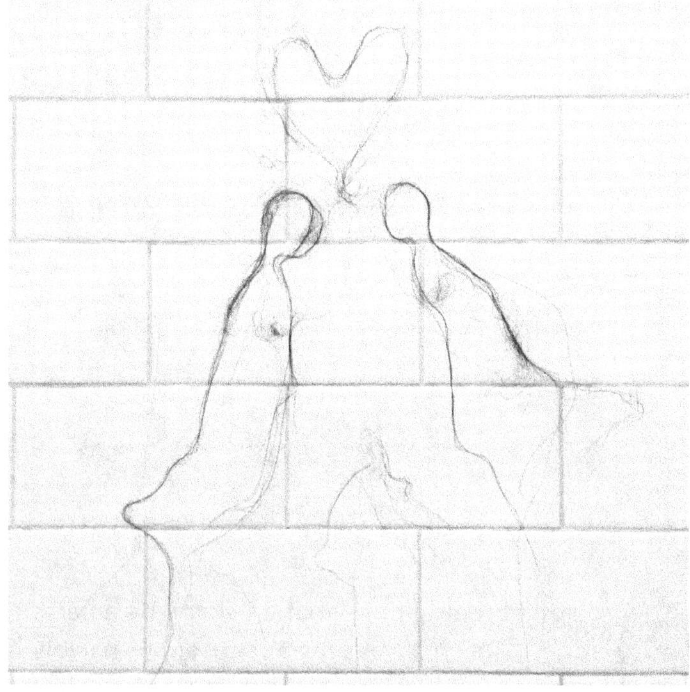

"Two Hearts"

It starts off just as a pair of lovers, friends. Maybe there is a long history together maybe it's all anew. You feel the pull of more waiting just beyond the brink of you two. The hope, the potential, the life that is awaiting. It's more than all the others before. This is the time the preverbal "one." I feel the pull for more. For more life, more time, more me, more you. You are told, "it won't be easy it will be hard, raising children and marriage is the hardest test of all." But you think it will be fine, it will be different for we two, we were destined. Nothing can rock us, shake us, no not to the core. We will learn though, if it does shake us, it shall be together. We will persevere through the peaks and valleys. Oh, my dears how there is much...much, much to learn.

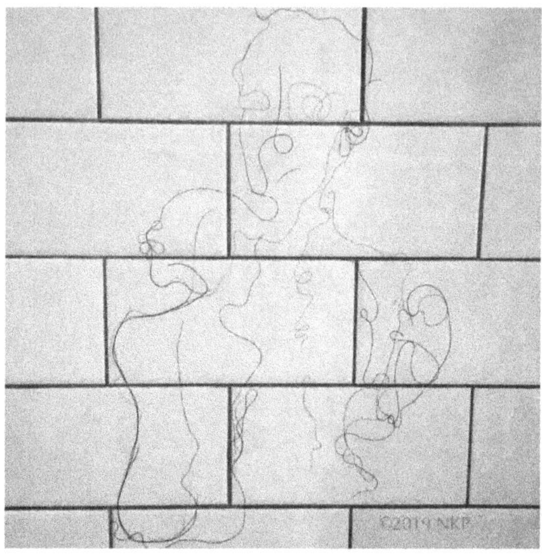

"Reality"

"You don't really know what it's like to be a parent until you are one." Which always made sense; but naively I believed "I understood" the undertaking of what motherhood meant. I "understood" that sacrifices would have to be made (naturally) and that it was just a normal part of becoming a parent. But nothing can quite prepare you for what is about to happen; even if it's something you have wanted your entire life.

I always knew I wanted to be a mother, I remember being 7 years old and actually telling my mum I wanted to be a mother when I grew up. And this was not a notion that was perpetuated by my parents. By no means at all. Both of my parents, especially being immigrants, were large proponents of my education. As a young girl born in the 80s, we were the generation of, "girls can grow up and be whatever they want to be." So, the desire for motherhood was always an intrinsic one. But I didn't understand just how much of one's self is lost in the process. And it has been a long road of processing and starting to come home to the self again...one that is still happening.

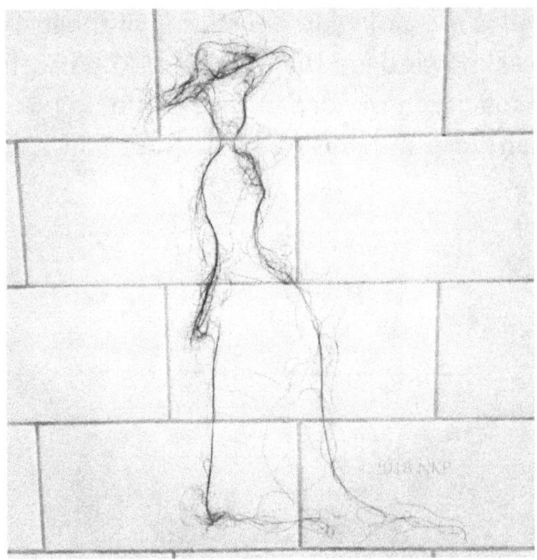

"Circa Turn of the Century"

There was a lot I didn't expect with the birth of my first son. Of course, how our lives would change, but I didn't realize that everything would be so scrutinized. How you are doing things, how you are not doing things, if you choose to want to have a life outside the home, if you choose to only have a life inside the home. The stroller you use, the clothes you put on your baby, the bottles you use, formula, no formula. The list goes on and on. Worst of all, I often felt the pressure from other mothers, not my peers, per se, but previous generations. There was always a sense that I felt like I was being judged for all my choices as a mother. And as my boy grew, it was how I was choosing to parent him that was" not right." As if there was some gatekeeper to the knowledge of parenthood, and the same people who said parenting didn't come with a manual all of a sudden made it seem like there was a manual...they had it and I didn't. What I would continue to have to fight for and earn later, was that I needed only to trust MYSELF and my way. Because, after all these are the children that the universe bestowed to me and I am the one charged with the guiding and nurturing of these children. No one else. I acknowledged that advice can be helpful at times, but the unsolicited opinions of those who do not, fully know my child, and are not raising him...those can see their way out.

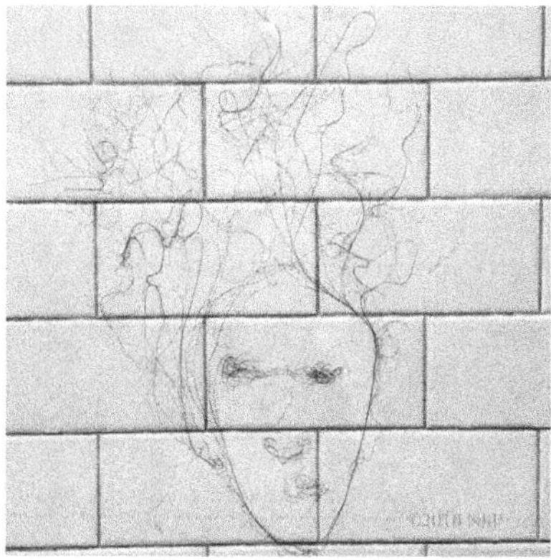

"The Chaos Within"

Thankfully, on my postpartum journey I did not experience the low, lows that I know some mothers experience; however, I was filled with what I now recognize as anxiety, rage, and frustration. I don't think I knew at times what was going on internally with me at all (and as a therapist who has gone through her own therapy...that's saying something). For so long survival mode seemed like the only way to go about daily life. I have always been told that I seem like a calm, chill person. So, I don't think I even realized what anxiety to that level even felt like until...truthfully...now. I so wish I knew then, what it was like to have a voice...how to talk to other mothers in a way that felt not like complaining or commiserating, but in an open and honest way. A way that showed how much I was struggling inside but didn't want to show "weakness" or that things were anything but "ALRIGHT." I know I didn't lie or present something not real, I just feel like I didn't speak my truth. I didn't always say, "it's been hard." Hell, I didn't share sometimes at all! Ever the listener, (job hazard) I always felt more comfortable holding space for others than for that space to be held for myself. Today, I am 6 years postpartum from my first birth and almost 3 from my second. It is only now, that the dust is finally settling. And with that I feel the chaos is finally starting to diminish. The noise within is starting to quiet and my voice- the voice of a women who has walked through different phases and stages of herself is finally starting to emerge.

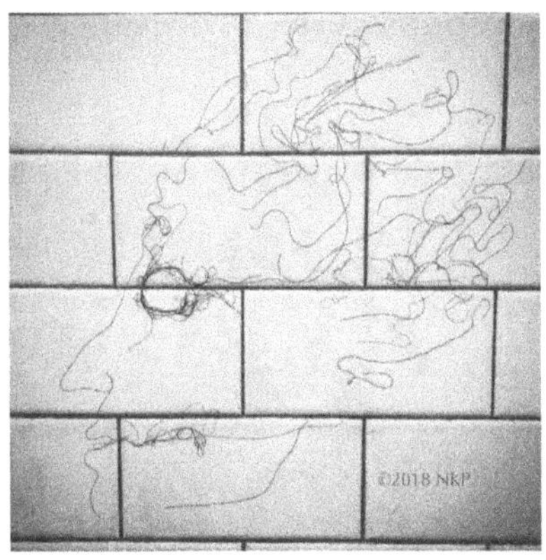

"Medusa"

<u>The Fire that Forged Me</u>
My tale isn't one of dragons slayed
or foes outweighed.
Nor, is it one of feats of grandeur
or spoils of war.
It is, in theory, a simple journey.
A task which many take.
But do not be fooled for in practice,
unlike in theory mistakes are easy to make.
Armed with only my courage of heart,
and little more than gumption;
I took to my charge, for it was at that junction-
I could've not known yet of the fire
that was to forge me.

The alchemy of time, to others might be trite
but to me there is no greater plight.
The comparison it might be said is
far too much made; but I beg to differ, for only now as I am
saved...
I recall a time of feeling in the trenches.
Deep in despair.
I wondered when will this end,
when will the night turn to dawn and
dispense with all my senses.

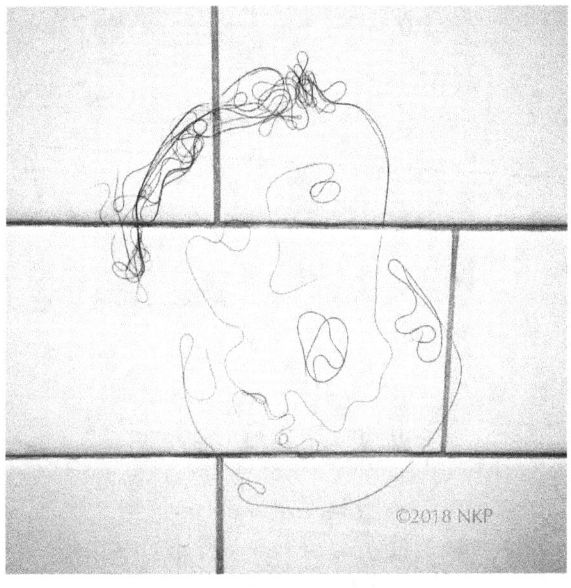

"Help"

The day I finally put up a call to help on FaceBook I felt I was at my wits end. I had been dealing with my back going out on and off for months after the birth of my second son. I was tired, in pain and drained; in need of more support than what my helpful mother could provide at the time. My longtime friend and fellow yoga instructor (we had met at a local yoga studio circa 2016 and had remained friends ever since) answered my cry saying, "if you are still in need of someone to help you, I would love to come and help you and your family." The absolute relief I felt when she messaged me... It was like rain in a drought. I could finally breathe again.

She came in and not only provided me with the sanity of adult conversation; but she loved on my son, fed me and my family with delicious healthy foods, helped me with laundry and generally picking up around the house. I felt like I was drowning and my friend was the life preserver I so badly needed. I couldn't have been more grateful for her, and to myself for having the courage to ask for help...which sometimes is just the HARDEST thing to do.

The other day my cousin from Australia whom, I will mention again later, messaged me. She is expecting her first child and (I'm sure her algorithms are aware of this.) She told me she stumbled upon a woman talking about being a postpartum doula. She said, "this sounds like what you have always wanted... a community, a village of people coming together to support a woman after she has had a child." And she couldn't have been more right.

After the birth of my second son I did have a postpartum doula. I knew I wanted a completely different postpartum experience the second time around than I had with the first. My first 40 days postpartum with my older son was wrought with isolation, anxiety and a lack of emotional support (not all of it of course but the key moments that stuck out.) So, the second time I knew, not only did I need, but I wanted, to be cocooned in a warm embrace. Especially by that of a female. My postpartum doula, in similar ways to my friend, came into my home, she would massage me with warm sesame seed oil for 90 minutes, would come bearing sustenance in the form of warm soups, roasted vegetables and more. Our conversations always left me feeling reassured. Her tender words and disposition, her being a mother herself, all aided me in seeing how mothers, not just our own, can give back to one another.

Of course, this did not come without cost, but it was more valuable to me than any material push present I could ever have imagined. I looked forward to her once a week visit. And when it was time for her to go after some weeks, I just remember my nervous system and psyche being in an utterly different state, then during my first 40 days with my older son.

What I learned from the two contrasting 4th trimester experiences are, what we seem to be missing in our culture. In a tribe or a village, our friends, mothers, sisters, aunts, grandmothers would come together and help a new mother handle the challenges of this great life shift. It is so essential to a woman, and her family. I can only imagine if this was a mainstream common occurrence in a family structure, what kind of ripples- what kind of vast changes would we see in our society? Would we be calmer, more well-adjusted? Would a slower pace of life creep back into the fold? Would neighborhoods feel more organic and safer? I don't know... but I dare to dream of how such community would shape our mothers, our women, our children. I feel like the wellbeing of the entire nucleus depends on how a new mother is cared for, especially in the first 40 days after her birth; the 4th trimester.

As I sit here and write I'm close to tears of gratitude. Without my postpartum doula, and my friend's help, I don't know where I would be. Both women eased my family into shifting from a unit of 3 to 4. And for that, both women will forever hold a special place in my heart.

Part 3
The Leveling Up

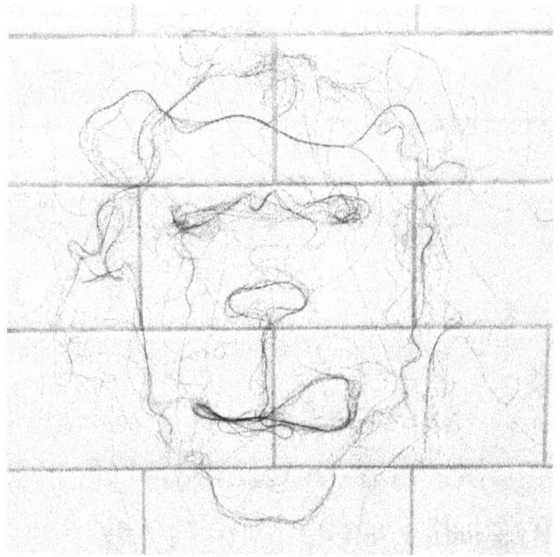

"Leo the Lion"

I'll never forget the day I "leveled up" nor when I was told, "You leveled up this year." The only time I had ever heard the expression was in reference to video games (not that I know anything about video games) but, if life trauma and near-death experiences are anything like getting to that next level in a video game then yeah; I would say I leveled up in 2023. The year started out with a New Year's Eve Trip to visit my dad's side of the family in Egypt. Growing up as a first generation American with both sides of my family literally living all over the world, I was fortunate enough to have traveled to see my grandparents, aunts, uncles and cousins for most of my youth. Thus, my goal for 2023 since our youngest was not yet 2, was to travel as much as possible without having to pay for 4 tickets. But in saving on our finances that year we

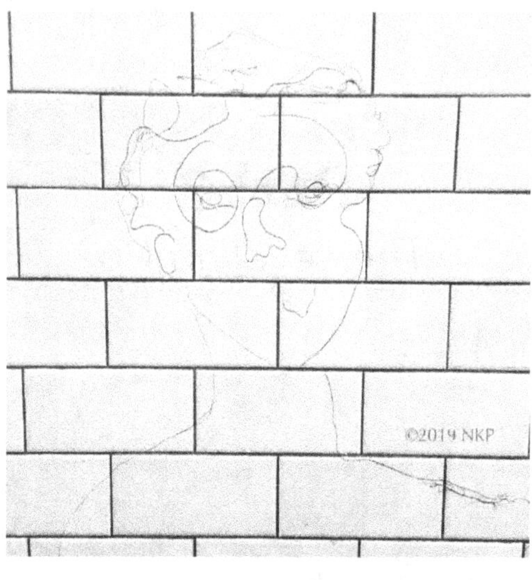

"The Little Guy"

paid the price in other ways. I was extremely excited though that my cousin (whom I mentioned before), who is more like a sister, from my mums' side of the family was making the trip all the way from Australia to meet us in Egypt as well. If it hadn't been a life goal of hers to visit Egypt; our family would have been irrevocably changed for the worse. The trip was wonderful, we got to see family, celebrate birthdays, even observe the Coptic Christmas (which my family celebrates on January 7th) ... until it was a parent's worst nightmare.

I've always loved the quote "If there is no mud, there can be no lotus" (I may be paraphrasing.) But the sentiment is always one that has stuck with me. If there are no hardships in life there can be no real beauty. Without adversity it is hard to rise up to a new level. Well the adversity surely came to us. Unbeknownst to us our youngest son was born with a genetic enzyme deficiency called G6PD. The irony is that we would have probably never discovered he had such a condition if we hadn't traveled to Egypt in the first place. How might you ask did we come to learn of this condition? Fava Beans...yes, the same ones that Hannibal Lecter enjoyed with a nice chianti and some liver. Those same fava beans were the culprit of a 3-day ICU stay, two blood transfusions, and countless needle sticks to our sweet 17-month-old. Not to mention being in a foreign country and not speaking the language (thank god for my family being there and translating.)

Falafel in Egypt, unlike most other Arab countries and in the US, is not made with chickpeas, but instead is made with fava beans. The particular enzyme that is found in fava beans is what our sons' body was unable to process, sending him into a hemolytic anemic reaction...basically all his red blood cells were exploding. All of this was the result of eating 3 Oreo size falafels and 2 days of decompensation. First, he became more lethargic, then jaundiced and if my cousin had not shown up when she did, which was 2 days after he had first eaten all the falafel, we would have lost my boy.

She having seen him healthy, and then seeing him in his current malady; snapped us into the critical nature of what was going on! He would not rebound from this without going to the hospital, he could not wait to go back to the states to get "our" health care...No, Stop, go to the hospital NOW. He will DIE if you don't. That's all I could hear my inner voice say. Even now sitting here and writing this, it is all so surreal.

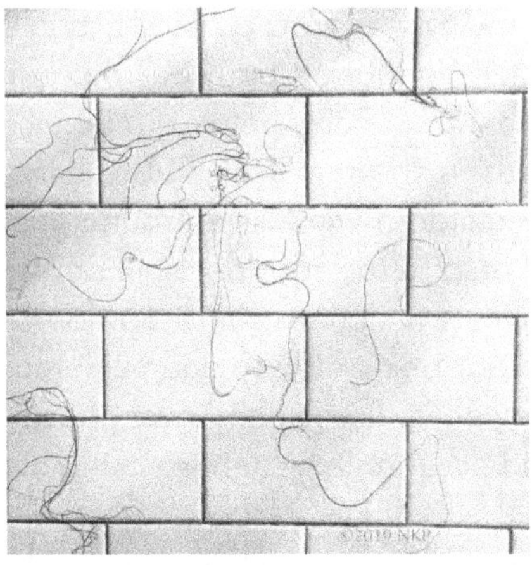

"The Onlook"

Thankfully our little cub is fine, no lasting stain on his life, other than certain medications that will always have to be avoided and fava beans...but as a mother, as a parent... what we went through...times when people in the hospital looked at us as if we were crazy for being beside ourselves (due to the commonplace of G6PD in the Mediterranean...at least that's what I told myself). The moment that my husband lost faith, and thought that this was it; I remember having to be strong, having to shake him like Cher in Moonstruck when she shakes Nicolas Cage, slaps him across the face and says, "Snap out of it" that was me telling him, "You can't lose hope! He will be fine once he gets the blood." But if I admit it, there was a moment I wasn't sure...and that's when I went to my phone and took a picture of our child. I thought if this is it, I want to remember. As morbid as that sounds, I didn't want to not have one last image of him. So, as he lay there in the hospital bed on oxygen as he was inches away from multiple organ failure; I took his picture.

Leveling up is taxing; it requires, at times, so much "holding it together" so much "strength" but damn is it EX-HAUSTING...I was so drained after the 3 days in the ICU. I stayed alone with him for the nights. During the day we had visitors; I am so grateful that not only did we have family there and my cousin from Australia but also my friend (the same one I mentioned before) from home came with us. My cousin and my friend helped to take care of our older son who was in the midst of all the pandemonium. My other cousins' children were also around and provided the much-needed respite for my older son. But the toll that this ordeal had on me, on all of us...I lost 8-10lbs in 3 days due to the stress and not being able to eat much more than boiled eggs; as I have celiac disease and every hospital meal came with pita bread or granola. When we came back home after the trip it was the first time, I truly cried...and it was a flood. I convulsed, I heaved and through it all we held each other, my husband and I. Finally, was I able to feel my feelings, allowed to bear the weight and realization of what happened. It was too much. It was relief and pain, fear and joy all at the same time. We had all come through on the other side. The lotus through the mud...the leveling up. What I didn't know at the time was that 2023 had more in store for me.

Part 4
The Leveling Up: Continued

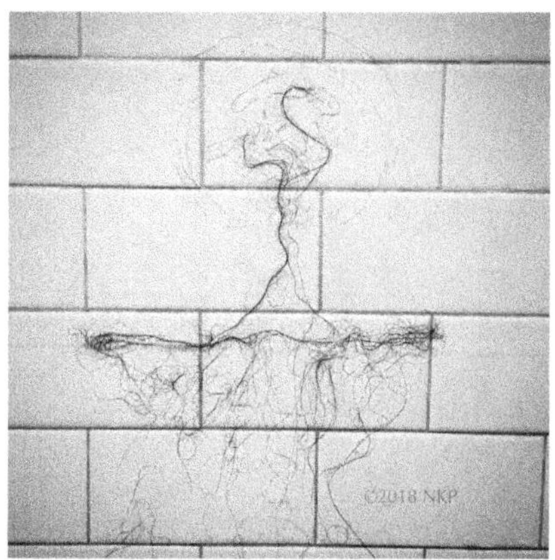

"In the Roots"

That summer was the second trip we embarked on. As my son would turn two in August, we decided to book our trip to Australia to see my mum's side of my family. But for this trip, my husband was not able to get the time off work as he started a new job just as we arrived back from Egypt. Which meant, you guessed it- I was taking both boys halfway around the world solo. Well...not entirely solo, my mum and stepdad would be accompanying me on the flights and would be staying with me and the boys at my aunt's house. Of course, traveling with family has its own share of challenges, as I'm sure any of you who have done it would understand. My aunt and grandmother as well as my several close cousins, including my cousin who came to Egypt with us, all live in Australia. I have to admit that before we even left for the trip, I was nervous; not because of what we experienced in Egypt; which naturally could have been a part of the anxiety. No, I could foresee some of the challenges I would face without my husband being with me on this journey. And that gave me pause. Still a young mother myself, I knew I was only truly as old as my oldest child when it came to my mothering skills...and I was learning how to parent in my own style and fashion. Just like a finger print; no two mothers are identical in how they choose to parent their children. I knew the way I chose and choose to mother is different from my mother's choosing. Not only for herself but also for how she saw I should execute the task. Unfortunately, my grandmother and I'm sure her mother and most likely a long line of women before her, my kin, were subjected to much female trauma, the kind of traumas that mark us to our core and shape our lives forever after; such scares stay within a family and can be passed down. These marks and scares were talked about fleetingly, in a way of matter of fact- these things happened, we lived with it...moving on. A remnant of the Old British stiff upper lip; it felt as though so much pain lies beneath the surface. If only we could have cried about it, held each other said I'm so sorry that happened to you and I love you. You should never have had to go through that...I wonder how that would have, if that even could have, changed things for others to come. Would it have softened the dispositions of those who were hardened? Would it have allowed for the healing to come sooner in the generational line, or not? I don't know but I do know that over time pain demands to be felt and dealt with. If not by those who directly were affected by an event, then by others. Other future female generations to come (at least in my family anyway). It always seems that the women bear the burden of feeling the pain and wrath; worst of all it coming from one another at times.

The constant judgement, critiquing, eyeing, weighing... the feeling of your mothering, your choices, what you do,

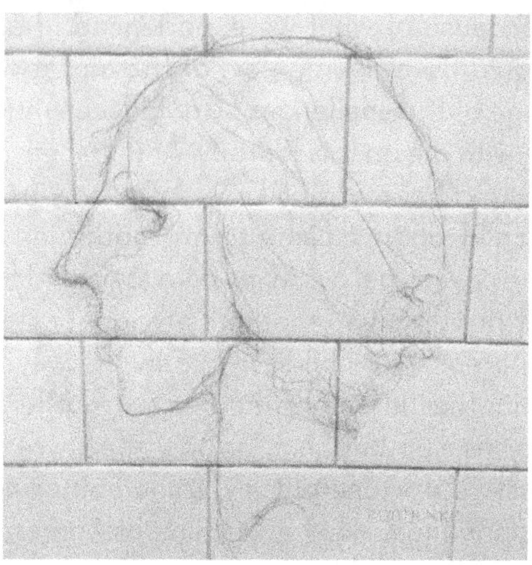

"The Woolf of it all"

say, if you discipline or not, the essence of you as a parent, constantly up for pecking.

For the 3 weeks that we were there, 9 of those days I had my cycle, I slept in the same bed as both my boys- thus very little sleep, was still nursing the little one, we went on 3 trips within the trip (therefore packing and repacking) my back going out, multiple fever blisters, and asthmatic attacks due to my severe dog and cat allergies. Not to mention the boy's "behavior" which was normal, however; with them not having their dad, multiple time changes, not the consistent routine of home, a new place, new people... and the ever-present judgement. When I tried to explain these reasons for why things were "less than ideal" what came into question was my mothering...these "reasons," were seen as "excuses." When I sought compassion, I felt I was met with lack of emotional support. I felt I was either expected to submit to being told I was not doing it right...therefore do it as you are supposed to...or I was left with no help. This was how I felt, how I perceived it. I know I had help from my cousins and my parents, but it was also with a side of judgement; just an extra little helping of criticism that always felt demoralizing. Why could it not just have been that this- what I was doing, bringing these children here to see their family- this is hard, you are doing your best. We see you and we love you... I did get some of that sentiment, at times it was there. We did have good moments on the trip, but the dye was already cast.

It took a lot out of me. I was emotionally depleted for the second time that year when I returned home. In fact, I was supposed to have gone to a wedding in Estonia (for a cousin on my dad's side) just 2 weeks after our return. Estonia was supposed to be the last trip right before our youngest turned 2 (literally to the day). It was supposed to be just me and him going this time. But, upon our return from Australia I told my dad I could not go. I could not take another family trip alone while single parenting; if just one thing had gone awry, I knew I would crack. Like a deep chasm in the earth, I would split in two. I feared my psyche wouldn't withstand the ordeal. So, I opted to put my own emotional and mental wellbeing above all else. And not go.

Not only did the trip take its toll on me emotionally but it also took a little bit for me to get back into a natural rhythm with my parents after Australia. Like I said before, such fires are needed for change. I know this to be all too true. In all that was said, the lacking that I felt at times, it was all necessary, necessary to get me to where I needed to go and to the path, I needed to be on in this life. I no longer harbor hurt or pain from the experience but instead I see how it was vital for me to arrive to where I am now. And while it took time to get here and to see that, it really was the greatest gift of all.

Part 5
The Healing

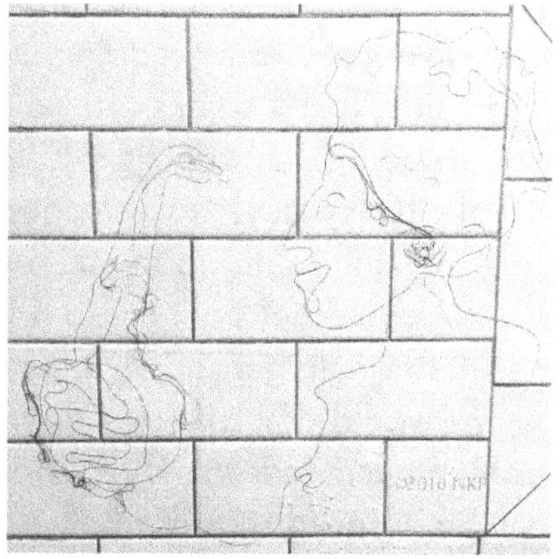

"The Serpent and Salt Lady"

I didn't even realize until I was writing this section just how beautiful the piece above is. It showed up on my shower wall in 2018, only to be truly realized 5 years later. And even further still, in the completeness of the journey now in 2024. I don't tend to believe in coincidence, I feel the universe sends us signs, pointing us in a direction, oftentimes only later do we realize the purpose. So, I really shouldn't be surprised at how prophetic this piece was.

Snakes, while seen by most as a sign of "evil" or "mistrust," are actually an ancient symbol of wisdom and knowledge. Of course, depending on who is writing the history and the agenda at hand; symbols always change with the tides and times. But that's what I have always been drawn to, not snakes per se, but knowledge, wisdom and the pursuit of truth. When I made this piece, I didn't particularly know why... I just did. Fast forward to 2023 (which by now you realize was a big one for me.) That October a longtime friend of mine messaged, asking if I would be interested in going to a sweat lodge with her at Hostel in the Forest in Brunswick, GA. I've known my friend since I was in elementary school; we went to middle and high school together reconnecting years later when we both moved back to our hometown in our mid-twenties. So, when she asked, I jumped at the opportunity to go. She had mentioned the hostel to me before and I always thought it sounded intriguing. I'll admit I haven't always been one for the great outdoors, mostly due to lack of exposure; but, in recent years, with the happenstance of having two very outdoorsy little boys I have become more open to discovering nature and all its splendor. Staying in a cabin with no A/C, no flushing toilets and outdoor showers was going to be easy- If I could go tent camping in the middle of a Florida summer with a 3-year-old, my husband and 7 months pregnant; I could do anything! Right?! The real test was going to be the sweat anyway.

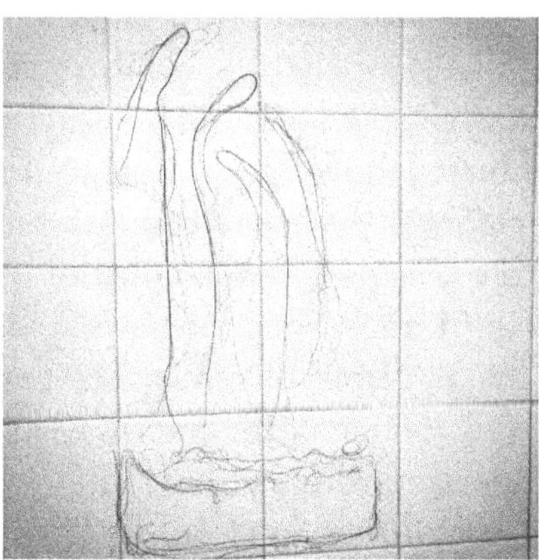

"In the Spirit of Dreams"

We arrived at the hostel the night before, to meet everyone participating in the sweat. The staff made us a dinner, which the hostel does every night. The food was so delicious and we had a communal clean up dance party after, which was epic. Once dinner was over, we sat by the fire and all discussed what we wanted to "get out" of the sweat. This was one of the most impactful parts for me. With that year having been such an odyssey it had opened my eyes to the inner work that needed to be done in my life. I spoke about letting go of feelings of judgement, and generational trauma. I felt heard, understood; held by this group of strangers. We were all here for something personal and different but nonetheless we all wanted to transform. After we all bared our souls, our Temezcal sweat leader saged us all with a resin from Mexico and then we all went to bed.

The next day was sweat day. Before the actual sweat we had to "build" the lodge. The lodge was basically a small dome frame made of bamboo, which we layered thick blankets over. The fire tenders of the sweat, they didn't actually participate in the sweat itself, built a fire to bake the 36 river stones that were need for the 4 rounds of the sweat. Totaling a time of 90 minutes to about 2 hours with 9 stones added to the pit each time the round began. When a round commenced the "door" would open to allow the stones to be brought in-this was the only time we were able to get fresh air to cool us down between rounds.

Before entering the lodge, a ritual to the 4 cardinal directions was performed followed by a prayer. Finally, before proceeding into our igloo of heat, all 24 of us pulled a card from an Aztec tarot deck, which the sweat leader provided. This is where things come full circle. The card I pulled was the Lady of the Salt- her Aztec name is Huixtocihuatl and she is often associated with serpents (the "being associated with serpents" I only learned as I was writing this- and I made "The Serpent and The Salt Lady" 6 years prior to pulling that card.) I found this particularly interesting because for the 4 rounds of the sweat, I was purging a LOT of salt.

For the first 2 rounds I balled my eyes out; literally having an inner dialogue with my self, that went something like-

"you can sit here in this heat and you can physically tough it out, or you can do the work, and if you really wanna do the work, you gotta let go girl...don't hold back you are in the dark womb now, if you wanna rebirth yourself here's your chance." As she beat the drum that marked the rounds of our transformation, as she sang and told us "this one is for the mother, your mother and all the women in your life," I wept like a woman in the depths of her grief. And when she said, "this one is for all the pain and fear you have held onto," I again cried and heaved, letting everything out. There was no holding back...I let the dam break; I knew it would be now or never, this was my chance to let it all go, finally having its moment to breathe. Like a bottle of wine corked for centuries, finally being released from its confinement. There was sweat, lots of tears, and a lot of snot; Did I mention lots of sweat?... We were packed pretty tightly in there and when we came out, it was literally like being reborn. We crawled out of the quilted doorway and as baby deer finding their new legs, stumbled out into the cool night air. Most of us made our way to the lake, and under the light of the full moon we swam, swam away the sweat, the tears and the snot. We swam ourselves clean. It was one of the most freeing moments of my life.

That weekend was also pivotal because it marked the first step, I made in a decision to dive into the deep inner workings of my psyche and soul. The day we left, Saturday, was the day I decided to sign up for a yearlong clairvoyant training.

Part 6
The Vision

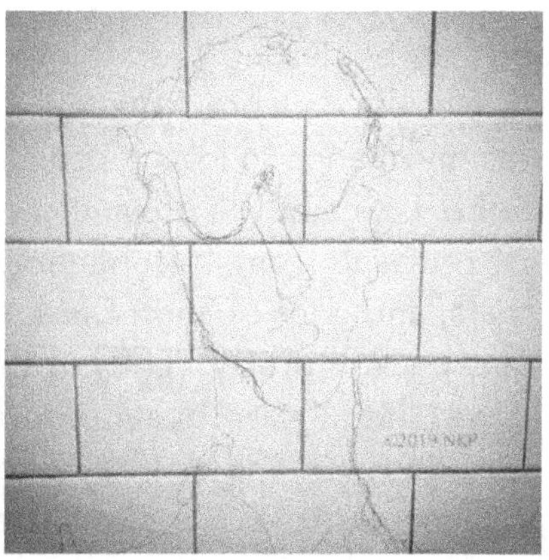

"Clear sight"

<u>The Musings of a Universe</u>
For the life I lead and creativity I breath.
I attribute all these gifts to the muse of the universe. Her
name whispers on the wind, Gaia, Isis, Shakti...long since
passed. I only know so above as below. I feel as though I've
been so many times before. For one thing I am certain this
classroom, this plane it is a lesson in learning.
For knowledge without growth is all for not.
And what would all this be if not for
...the musings of a universe.

How it came to be that I ended up in a clairvoyant training is
much like how it came to be that I went to the sweat lodge.
The "Clear Sight" piece again was an unknowing prophecy.

In July of 2023 after I came back from Australia, and well before the sweat lodge; I hosted a Tarot card reading event with a friend of a friend who happened to be a tarot card reader and intuitive.

But it just so happened that, that same weekend one of my best friends from high school was in town from Atlanta. I told her that if she was able to make it to the event that I would love to have her there. She said she would try as it sounded super interesting. Honestly, I was a little surprised- in high school she was more on the reserved side, but I believe that was more due to family ties. Thrilled nonetheless I hoped she would make it. So, when she turned up, I was excited and still slightly stunned that the conservative girl from our high school days was there...prime example of how one can evolve over time.

She was always a magical person though, so bubbly and full of life, she was always up to have fun, just a sunshine on a cloudy day type of person. But when she said she got interested in tarot because of a cousin who is a psychic, and teaches at a clairvoyant school...I about fell out of my chair... I was dumbfounded! "You have a cousin who...? What?!

Seeing my obvious intrigue, she put the two of us in touch. Her cousin and I ended up collaborating and offering a New Moon meditation circle that was virtual as well as local. It was pretty cool (if I do say so myself.)

I ended up getting a reading from her cousin and then learned more about the school. From there I attended one of the schools open houses, and then stewed on it for a while. Months in fact. All until that weekend in October when I made the pivotal decision.

The whole point of this explanation on how I ended up coming to clairvoyant school is really with one cord that ties everything together. It was a way to come back to my TRUE self. Free from the judgment. Free from what others would think of me, if I decided to do this course. Truthfully, I no longer cared what family would think, or anyone else. I needed to do this for me. I needed to follow my heart, my interests, my instincts. I needed to get me back. The me that was always interested in the magic of life, the beauty, the harmony and the truth of it. To see that girl...nay woman, without fear or critique, just as she is.

Free to be herself. Despite her role as mother, wife, daughter. For first I am a woman, a person, a being... who just wants to be.

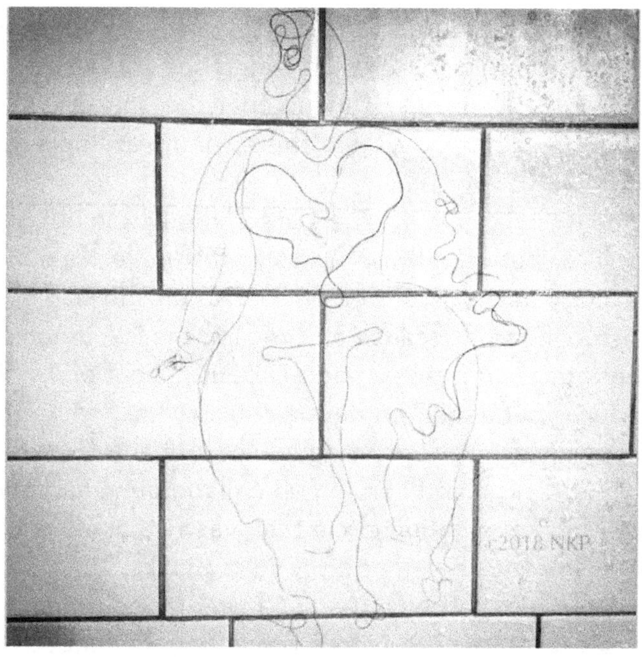

" Venus in all her Glory"

Part 7
The Voice

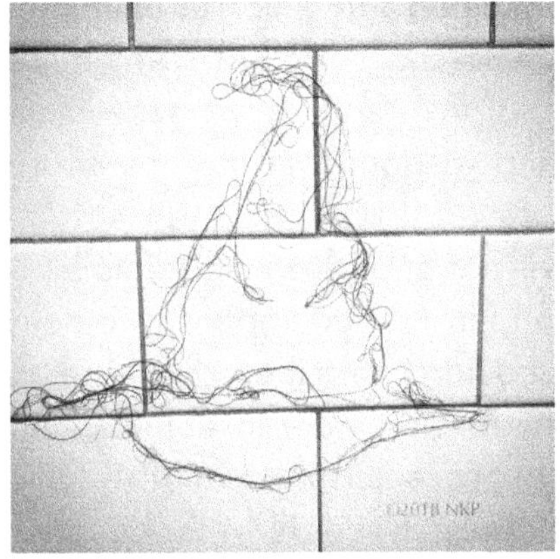

"The Sorting Hat"

Uncovering my true self, which is forever a discovery (and I don't believe by any means is "now over") has been some of the best work I have done to this point in my life. The best creations of my life have been my children, but the best work I have done, that has been on myself. All this growth of course will be benefited by my children. It is hard work, it has had its challenges but it has been so rewarding; and it continues to be. I don't believe I would have had the courage to find my voice and write this book, which is something I always wanted to do, if I hadn't started to excavate who I am from the recesses of my spirit.

I remember being in 6th grade and telling my English teacher when she asked the class "what do you want to be when you grow up? That I want to be a writer. Over the years though that spark of my bold gumption dimmed. I have always loved being creative and the arts, (as mentioned before) but to call myself an artist, a writer....no, no, no I could not do *that*... that title was for serious creatives; people who had made the choice to go to art school, whose artwork and talent was undeniable. People whose paintings were so life-like you could reach out and grab it; whose writing was published in books and magazines.

Now, lately, I feel the call, the pull to go back to that wide-eyed girl who was so full of so many feelings, of sadness, of magic, of love and happiness. Inspired by her but with the age and wisdom that life has afforded me. Now I want to boldly say: I AM A WRITER, I AM AN ARTIST, I AM CREATIVE. I will not back down and simply be pregnant with ideas but be too fearful, too impotent to deliver them (I see the pun there...couldn't pass it up.) I will rise up, I will succeed and I do have faith; faith in me, in womenkind, in mothers old and new, in my children, in my family and in the universe. It is so for it has always been...Now is the moment, this is the time, this is and was always the time that my younger self has been waiting for. I realize you young girl so fresh at only 11 years old, you have waited all this time but now you have arrived...you are a writer now. When the day comes that you are able to see your creation, our creation come to life in black and white; we will rejoice together! Know this though dear girl, despite this achievement the biggest one of all has been seeing you. The REAL you. Finding her, loving her and helping her. That has been the greatest joy and work of my, OUR, life to date. Dear girl, daughter, woman, mother. My dearest loved one. I am PROUD of you...I am proud of all that you do, for all that you are and for all that you/we are becoming. Now and for always. Know that I see you and I love you; you have found your voice now...continue to share it and be heard.

Author's Note

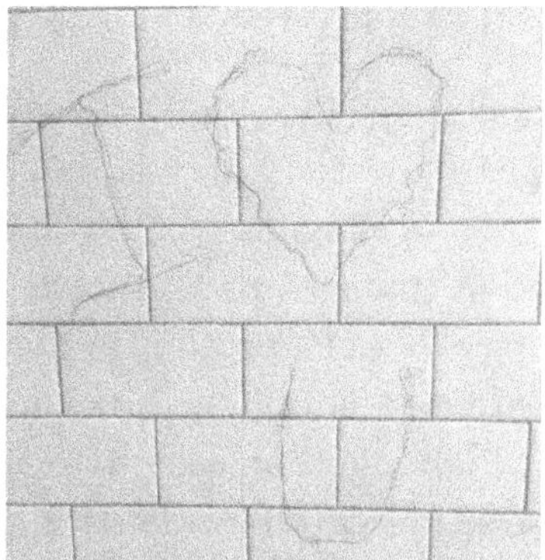

I just wanted to say thank you to all of you who have read my work. I truly hope, small though it may be, that these words and this experience has brought something to your life. To my friends and family, I want to say sincerely from the bottom of my heart...thank you for your love and support, not just with the creation of this book but in my life, in general. I am so grateful for all of you and your belief in me.

Love always,
Natasha

About The Author

Natasha K. Preckajlo is a Licensed Clinical Social Worker, and certified yoga instructor. She has had her own private practice since 2019 and remains an active healer to this day. Always interested in the arts, dance, creativity and writing; She began creating more after the birth of her first son, and continues to learn more about the spiritual journey that is motherhood and life. Together with her two sons and her husband she resides in North Florida. This is her first book.